Insect Pollinators

by Jennifer Boothroyd

first step nonfiction

Lerner Publications · Minneapolis

LERNER

SOURCE™

Expand learning beyond the printed book. Download free, complementary educational resources for this book from our website, www.lernerresource.com.

The images in this book are used with the permission of: © iStockphoto.com/proxyminder, p. 4; © iStockphoto.com/antb, p. 5; © iStockphoto.com/aimintang, p. 6; © iStockphoto.com/JLF Capture, p. 7; © herreid/iStock/Thinkstock, p. 8; © iStockphoto.com/Lingbeek, p. 9; © iStockphoto.com/SeaDog53, p. 10; © NagyDodo/Thinkstock, p. 11; © Andalucia Plus Image Bank/Alamy, p. 12; © Dragi52/iStock/Thinkstock, p. 13; © Ingram Publishing/Thinkstock, p. 14; © Michael and Patricia Fogden/Minden Pictures/Getty Images, p. 15; © Mishell/iStock/Thinkstock, p. 16; © Konrad Wothe/Minden Pictures/Getty Images, p. 17; © iStockphoto.com/Kirshal, p. 18; © Ingram Publishing/Thinkstock, p. 19; © iStockphoto.com/njmcc, p. 20; © Therry/iStock/Thinkstock, p. 21; © Fuse/Thinkstock, p. 22. Front cover: © iStockphoto.com/tcp.

Main body text set in ITC Avant Garde Gothic Std Medium 21/25.
Typeface provided by Adobe Systems.

Lerner Publications Company
A division of Lerner Publishing Group, Inc.
241 First Avenue North
Minneapolis, MN 55401 USA

For reading levels and more information, look up this title at www.lernerbooks.com.

Library of Congress Cataloging-in-Publication Data

Boothroyd, Jennifer, 1972–
     Insect pollinators / by Jennifer Boothroyd.
          pages   cm. — (First step nonfiction. Pollination)
     Includes index.
     ISBN 978–1–4677–5738–6 (lib. bdg. : alk. paper)
     ISBN 978–1–4677–6225–0 (eb pdf)
     1. Insect pollinators—Juvenile literature. 2. Pollination—Juvenile literature. I. Title. II. Series:
First step nonfiction. Pollination.
     QK926.B66 2015
     576.8′75—dc23   2014015506

Manufactured in the United States of America
4 - 45777 - 17872 - 4/4/2019

Table of Contents

Pollination

This bee is busy. It is gathering food.

Pollen is powder inside a flower.

The bee is also helping the plant. The bee is moving **pollen**.

5

Pollination is when pollen moves between parts of flowers.

How Do Insects Pollinate?

All **insects** pollinate plants in similar ways.

Pollen often sticks to an insect's back, legs, or head.

First, an insect crawls on a flower. Pollen sticks to the insect.

8

The pollen rubs off the insect onto the milkweed flower.

Next, the insect moves to a different flower. The pollen falls onto the flower.

Milkweed seeds blow in the wind.

Then the flower uses the pollen to make **seeds**.

Kinds of Insect Pollinators

Many different kinds of insects pollinate plants.

There is a lot of pollen on this beetle.

Beetles pollinate.

Lacewings pollinate.

Butterflies pollinate.

Butterflies have **bristles** on their legs that carry pollen.

Moths pollinate.

This hawk moth is feeding on a flower.

Some moths pollinate flowers that bloom at night.

Wasps pollinate.

Flies pollinate.

Protecting Pollinators

Some **pollinators** are in trouble. They are dying out.

Apple, pear, and peach trees need bees.

Much of the food we eat comes from plants pollinated by bees.

These children have a bee-friendly garden.

It is important to protect pollinators.

Glossary

bristles – short, stiff hairs

insects – animals that do not have backbones. Insects have three body sections; three pairs of legs; and, typically, wings.

pollen – a yellowish powder made inside flowers

pollination – the transfer of pollen from one part of a flower to another part of a flower of the same kind

pollinators – animals that pollinate flowers

seeds – parts of flowering plants that are able to grow new plants

Index